PSALM 91

God's Umbrella of Protection

PEGGY JOYCE RUTH

Psalm 91
God's Umbrella of Protection

Printed in the United States of America by
Morris Publishing
3212 E. Hwy 30
Kearney, NE 68847
800 650 7888
http://morrispublishing.com

Additional copies may be ordered from:

Peggy Joyce Ruth BETTER LIVING Ministries
P.O. Box 1549, Brownwood, Texas, 76804-1549
    Phone: 915 646-6894; Fax: 915 643-9772

ISBN 0-9716978-0-9

First Printing . 5000 copies. December, 2001

With special thanks to:
Design by Joseph Dispensa of Galway, Ireland
        and Sandi Brown of Brownwood, Texas
Cover by Marcus Stallworth of Dallas, Texas.
Edit by Eloise Wright of Irving, Texas

TABLE OF CONTENTS

Foreword		5
Introduction		7
Setting the Scene		9
Chapter 1	Where is my dwelling place?	15
Chapter 2	What am I saying?	21
Chapter 3	Deliverance by man is in vain!	26
Chapter 4	Under His wings!	30
Chapter 5	A mighty fortress is My God!	32
Chapter 6	I will not fear the terror!	34
Chapter 7	I will not fear the arrow!	41
Chapter 8	I will not fear the pestilence!	44
Chapter 9	I will not fear the destruction!	48
Chapter 10	Though a thousand fall...	52
Chapter 11	No plague comes near my family!	59
Chapter 12	Angels watching over me!	63
Chapter 13	The enemy under my feet!	67
Chapter 14	Because I love Him...	73
Chapter 15	God is my deliverer!	75
Chapter 16	I am seated with Christ Jesus!	77
Chapter 17	God answers my call!	81
Chapter 18	God rescues me from trouble!	87
Chapter 19	God honors me!	90
Chapter 20	God satisfies me with long life!	93
Chapter 21	I behold His Salvation!	95
Summary		97
What must I do to be Saved?		99
Testimonies		102

FOREWORD

In the midst of these turbulent times, God has anointed Peggy Joyce to write this wonderful book, *Psalm 91: God's Umbrella of Protection.*

When someone has walked in a Truth of God for over 30 years, there is a depth of insight incomparable to anything else. Such is the case of Peggy Ruth, our dear friend and partner in the ministry. What a gift she is to the Body of Christ! She is a Pastor's wife, Bible teacher, radio host and author. And there is no fluff to Peggy! She is Rock solid and has earned the right to be listened to. From her personal furnace of affliction, she has effectively explained this infamous Psalm and challenged us to new levels of faith and trust in God.

This is more than an inspiring book. It is a parent's manual, a leader's handbook, a pastor's promise and a Christian's covenant. I wholeheartedly recommend this book. It contains both inspiration and information which remains Biblically sound.

Along with this much needed book, Tommy and I applaud both Jack and Peggy Joyce for their unwavering faithfulness to their many assignments from the Lord. Their lives are a book!

Rachel Burchfield
President of Texas Bible Institute

INTRODUCTION

Are you tired of tormenting fear thoughts that seem to always be lurking just below the surface, ready to control your life and steal your peace and well being? If so, I think you will find that the message in this book is the answer you've been searching for.

Maybe you fear the dangers that face your children everyday — peer pressure, drugs or alcohol. I, too, faced those fears. I also used to battle the nagging anxiety about what I would do if my husband, Jack, was in a car wreck, had a sudden heart attack or was involved in some other tragedy that might claim his life.

Those fears that tormented my imagination used to be my constant companions. Yet it was easy to justify them with all that was going on in the world!

Back in the 1950's things were fairly predictable, but the word *predictable* was becoming more obsolete with each passing decade. Fear was running rampant because of the uncertainty of the times—cancer, natural disasters, financial difficulties and terrorism were everywhere I turned. But after all, didn't the Bible tell us in Matthew 24, that in the last days, *"Men's hearts would fail because of fear?"* Somehow it consoled me to know that I was not alone in my dilemma.

But one Sunday changed everything. That's the day the Lord miraculously, through a dream, spoke to me and answered my question— "Is there any way to be protected from all the things that are coming on the earth?" When I awoke, peace—like warm oil—flowed over me.

But it wasn't until the next day that I discovered that the words God spoke to me were found in verse 15 of Psalm 91. That is when I began to study Psalm 91 as though my very life depended on it. And I realized that Psalm 91 was not just something to bring comfort to me during times of sorrow. I saw that it was there to take me *victoriously* through any crisis I might encounter.

This book is the result of the longing in my heart to help people who are struggling with the same fears that I agonized over for so long. If this is something you already know, then God wants to remind you of this truth.

I encourage you to mark these scriptures in your own Bible as we go straight through this Psalm. This is God's *covenant umbrella of protection* for you personally.

My prayer is that Psalm 91 will give you the **COURAGE TO TRUST!**

Setting the scene

Sundays were usually a comfort. For some reason being inside the church building made the fears temporarily disappear—but not on this particular Sunday!

Our pastor looked unusually serious that day as he made the announcement that one of our most beloved and faithful deacons had been diagnosed with leukemia and had only a few weeks to live. Only the Sunday before, this robust-looking deacon in his mid-forties had been in his regular place in the choir — looking as healthy and happy as ever. Now, one Sunday later, the entire congregation was in a state of shock after hearing such an unexpected announcement.

Several of the members got upset with the pastor when he said, "Get out all of your silly little get-well cards and start sending them." But I completely understood the frustration that had initiated that remark. However, little did I know that this incident would pave the way to a *MESSAGE THAT WAS GOING TO FOREVER BURN IN MY HEART.*

Surprisingly, I had gone home from church that day feeling very little fear, perhaps because I was numb from the shock of what I had heard. I vividly remember sitting down on the edge of the bed that afternoon and saying out loud, "Lord, is there any way to be protected from all the evils that are coming on the earth?"

I was not expecting an answer. I was merely voicing the thought that kept going over and over in my mind. I remember lying across the bed and falling immediately to sleep, only to wake up a short five minutes later. However, in those five minutes I had a very unusual dream.

In the dream I was in an open field asking the same question that I had prayed earlier — "Is there any way to be protected from all the things that are coming on the earth?" And in my dream I heard these words:

> *"In your day of trouble call upon Me, and I will answer you!"*

Suddenly, I knew I had the answer I had so long been searching for. The ecstatic joy I felt was beyond anything I could ever describe. And instantly, to my surprise, there were hundreds of Christians with me in the dream out in that open field, praising and thanking God for the answer.

But it wasn't until the next day when I heard the 91st Psalm referred to on a tape by Shirley Boone, that suddenly I *knew in my heart* that *whatever* was in that Psalm was God's answer to my question. I nearly tore up my Bible in my haste to see what it said. And there it was in verse 15—the *exact statement* that God had spoken to me in my dream. I could hardly believe my eyes!

I believe that you who are reading this book are among the many Christians who were pictured with me in that open field, who will, through the Message in this book, get your answer to the question, "Can a Christian be protected through these turbulent times?"

Since the early 1970's, I have had many opportunities to share this message. I feel that God has commissioned me to write this book to proclaim God's *Covenant of Protection*. May you be sincerely blessed by it.

Peggy Joyce Ruth

Psalm 91

He who dwells in the shelter of the Most High
Will abide in the shadow of the Almighty.
I will say to the Lord, "My refuge and my fortress,
My God, in whom I trust!"
For it is He who delivers you from the snare of the trapper,
And from the deadly pestilence.
He will cover you with His pinions,
And under His wings you may seek refuge;
His faithfulness is a shield and bulwark.

You will not be afraid of the terror by night,
Or of the arrow that flies by day;
Of the pestilence that stalks in darkness,
Or of the destruction that lays waste at noon.
A thousand may fall at your side,
And ten thousand at your right hand;
But it shall not approach you.
You will only look on with your eyes,
And see the recompense of the wicked.
For you have made the Lord, my refuge,
Even the Most High, your dwelling place.

No evil will befall you, nor will any plague come near your tent.
For He will give His angels charge concerning you,
To guard you in all your ways.
They will bear you up in their hands,
Lest you strike your foot against a stone.
You will tread upon the lion and cobra,
The young lion and the serpent you will trample down.

Because he has loved Me, therefore I will deliver him;
I will set him securely on high, because he has known My name.
He will call upon Me, and I will answer him;
I will be with him in trouble; I will rescue him, and honor him.
With a long life I will satisfy him,
And let him behold My salvation.

Chapter 1

He who dwells in the shelter of the Most
High will abide in the shadow of the Almighty.
-Psalm 91:1

Have you ever been inside a cabin
with a big roaring fire in the fireplace, en-
joying this wonderful feeling of safety and
security as you watched an enormous elec-
trical storm going on outside? It was a
warm, wonderful sensation knowing that
you were being sheltered and protected
from the storm. That is what Psalm 91 is
all about!

Did you know that there is a place in
God—a secret place—for His children who
want to seek refuge? **There is a literal**

place of physical safety and security that God tells us about in this psalm.

I am sure that every one of you can think of something that represents *security* to you. When I think of security and protection, I have a childhood memory that automatically comes to mind. It revolves around my parents taking me and my younger brother and sister out to a lake to fish for an afternoon of fun.

Dad had a secluded place on this lake near Brownwood where he would take us to fish for perch. That was the second greatest highlight of the outing. I loved seeing the cork begin to bobble, and then suddenly it would go completely out of sight. There were only a few things that could thrill me more than jerking back on that old cane pole and landing a huge perch right in the boat.

I think I was grown before I realized that Dad had an ulterior motive in taking us for an afternoon of perch fishing. Those perch were his bait for the trotline that he had stretched out across one of the secret coves at the lake.

Dad would drive the boat over to the place where his trotline was located, then he would cut off the boat motor and inch the boat across the cove as he "ran the trot line." That's what he called it when he would hold onto the trotline with his hands and pull the boat alongside all the strategically placed, baited hooks to see if any of them had hooked a large catfish.

I said that catching the perch was the *second* greatest highlight of the outing. By far the greatest thrill was the times when Dad would get to a place where the trotline rope would begin to jerk almost out of his hand. It was then that we three siblings would watch — wide eyed — as Dad would wrestle with that line until finally in victory he would flip that huge catfish over the side of the boat right in the floor board at our feet. Money couldn't buy that kind of excitement! The circus and carnival, all rolled up into one, couldn't compete with that kind of a thrill.

One of these outings proved more

eventful than most—turning out to be an experience that I will never forget. It had been a beautiful day when we started out, but by the time we had finished our perch fishing and were headed toward the cove, everything changed. A storm came up on the lake so suddenly that there was no time to get back to the boat dock. The sky turned black, lightning was flashing, and drops of rain were falling with such force that they actually stung when they hit. Then moments later we began to be pelted by large marble-sized hailstones.

I could see the fear in my mother's eyes, and I knew we were in danger. But before I had time to wonder what we were going to do, Dad had driven the boat to the rugged shoreline of the only island on the lake. Boat docks surround that island now, but then it just looked like an abandoned island with absolutely no place to take cover.

In just moments, Dad had us all out of the boat and ordered the three of us to lie down beside our mother on the ground. Quickly pulling a canvas tarp out of the bottom of the boat, he knelt down on the ground beside us and pulled that tarp up over all five of us. He had fashioned a tent over us. And as that storm raged on outside, we were secure and safe under the protection of the shield my father had provided.

In fact, I had never felt as safe and secure in my entire life. I can remember thinking that I wished that the storm would last forever. I didn't want anything to spoil the wonderful security that I felt that day—there *in our secret hiding place*. Feeling my father's protective arms around me, I never wanted it to end.

I have never forgotten that experience, but today it has taken on new meaning. Just as Dad had put a tarp over us that day to shield us from the storm, our Heavenly Father has a *Secret Place* in Himself that will protect us from the storms that are raging out there in the world around us.

That *Secret Place* is literal, but it is also conditional! And here in verse one God lists our part of the condition before He even mentions the promises included in

His part. That's because *our part* has to come first. In order to abide in the *shadow* of the Almighty, we must *choose to dwell* in the shelter of the Most High.

The question is—"How do we dwell in the shelter of the Most High?" We dwell in His shelter by believing that He is a literal place of refuge where we can be physically protected when we are willing to run to Him.

You might call that *place of refuge*—a *Love Walk*! It is actually a relationship with the Father that you have cultivated and developed in this *secret place,* by investing enough time into it to make it very personal and intimate.

Chapter 2

I will say to the Lord, "My Refuge and my Fortress, my God, in whom I trust!" -Psalm 91:2

We must choose to see God literally as *our Refuge — our Fortress — our God — the One in whom we trust!* We have to make Him our Source.

Notice that verse two says, "I will say..." Circle the word *"say"* in your Bible because we must learn to verbalize our *trust* out loud. It is not enough to just *think* it. The scripture says that we must *say* it.

There is something about saying it that releases power in the spiritual realm.

Notice what begins to happen on the inside when you start saying, "Lord, You are my Refuge — You are my Fortress — You are my Lord and my God! It is in You that I put my total trust!" The more we say that out loud, the more confident we become in His protection.

So many times as Christians, we mentally agree that the Lord is our Refuge — but that is not good enough. *Power is released* in saying it out loud. When we begin to say it and mean it, we are placing ourselves in His shelter. By voicing *His Lordship* and *His Protection*, we open the *door* to the secret place.

God knows that He has to be our Source before the promises in Psalm 91 will ever work because Psalms 60:11b tells us *"...deliverance and protection by man is in vain."* Have you ever tried to protect yourself from all the bad things that can happen? It's like trying to keep the whole law. God knows we can't do it.

We could go to the doctor once a month for a checkup. We could double check our cars every day to see that the motor, the tires and the brakes were all in good running order. We could fireproof our houses and store up food for a time of need. Yet we still couldn't do enough to protect ourselves from every potential danger. It's impossible!

Not that any one of these precautions is wrong. It is just that none of these things, in and of themselves, has the power to protect. God has to be the One to whom we run first. **He is the only One who has an answer for *whatever* might come.**

When I think of how utterly impossible it is to protect ourselves from all the evils that are in the world, I always think of a sheep. A sheep has no real protection other than its shepherd. In fact, it is the only animal I can think of that has *no* built-in protection. It has no sharp teeth, no offensive odor to spray to drive off its enemies, no loud bark, and it certainly can't run fast enough to get away.

Maybe that's why the Bible calls us God's sheep! God is saying, "I want you to see Me as your Source of protection. I am your Shepherd." Now He may use doctors, storm cellars and bank accounts to meet our needs, but our hearts have to run to Him first as our Shepherd and our Protector. Then *He* will choose the method He desires to bring about the protection.

How often I've heard people say, "I can't dwell in the shelter of God. I mess up and fall short too many times. I feel guilty and unworthy." God knows all about our weaknesses. That's why He gave His Son. We can no more earn this protection, or deserve it, than we can earn or deserve our salvation.

Don't point to what you've done or haven't done. Point to what Jesus has done for you. **We dwell in His shelter by faith in God's grace.** And faith is not hard. It is simply our positive response to what Jesus has already provided through His Blood .

We cannot perform enough good deeds to keep ourselves in His shelter anymore than we can do enough to keep ourselves saved. We have to realize that we dwell in His shelter—not in our own righteousness, but in the Righteousness of Jesus Christ.

We could never be good enough on our own. Our righteousness and our own efforts will never measure up. It's His mercy that makes all of this possible— giving us not what we deserve, but what we don't deserve—through the Blood of Jesus.

> For by His doing, you are in Christ
> Jesus who became to us wisdom
> From God, and righteousness ...
> —I Corinthians 1: 30

There is a difference, however, between making an occasional mistake and staying in willful sin. Self-will and rebellion will keep us out of the secret place of protection because self-will is a wall that we build between God and us.

Our part is expressed in verses one and two. For as we allow Him to be the Lord of our lives, His power is released to bring about the promises found in verses three through 16. Our part is small, but necessary, to release His part of the Covenant.

Chapter 3

For it is He who delivers you from the snare of the trapper and from the deadly pestilence.   —Psalm 91: 3:

As hard as we may try, we can never deliver ourselves from the snare of the trapper. It is He (God) who will deliver us. As we said in Chapter 2 "deliverance by man is in vain." The *snare of the trapper* is just a graphic way of explaining the adversary — the enemy, Satan — the thief, as Jesus called him in John 10:10.

Have you ever seen a movie where a fur trapper would go up deep into the mountains in the cold climate, bait big steel traps, cover them over with leaves and then wait for some unsuspecting animal to step into the trap? Those traps were not there by chance. The trapper had taken great care to place them in very strategic locations.

Well, that is a picture of what the enemy does to us. That's why he is called the *trapper!* The traps that are set for us are not there by accident. They are custom made, placed and baited specifically for each one of us.

The enemy knows exactly what will most likely hook us, and he knows exactly which *thought* to put into our minds to lure us into the trap. That is why Paul tells us in 2 Corinthians 2: 11 that we are *"...not to be ignorant of the schemes (traps) of the enemy."* Then he says:

> For the weapons of our warfare are not of the flesh, but divinely powerful for the destruction of fortresses. We are destroying speculations and every lofty thing raised up against the knowledge of God, and we are taking every thought captive to the obedience of Jesus Christ.
> —2 Corinthians 10:4–5

God not only delivers us from the snare laid by the trapper, but according to the last part of verse three, He also delivers us from the deadly *pestilence*. I always thought that a pestilence was something that attacked crops — like bugs, locusts, grasshoppers, spider mites, mildew and root rot. But after doing a word study on the word *pestilence*, I found, to my surprise, that pestilence attacks people — not crops!

Webster's New World Dictionary says that pestilence is *"any virulent or fatal disease; an epidemic that hits the masses of people-- any deadly disease that attaches itself to one's body with the intent to destroy."* But God says, "I will deliver you from the deadly disease that comes with the intent to destroy."

Do we as Christians even stop to consider what this is saying to us? Do we have the courage to trust God's Word enough to believe that He means this literally? Is it possible for it to be true, and yet still miss out on these promises?

There were many lepers in Israel in the time of Elijah, but Jesus said in Luke 4: 27, *"None of them was cleansed."* Only Naaman, the Syrian, was healed when he obeyed in faith. Not everyone will receive the benefits of this promise in Psalm 91. Only those who believe God and hold fast to His promises will profit—but none-the-less, it *is* available.

Chapter 4

He will cover you with His pinions, and under His wings, you may seek refuge.
—Psalm 91: 4a

Did you notice that it says that He will cover you with His pinions (feathers) and under His wings, you *may* seek refuge? Again, it's up to us to make that decision! We can seek refuge under His wings, if we choose to.

The Lord gave me a very vivid picture of what it means to seek refuge under His wings. My husband, Jack, and I live out in the country, and one spring our old mother hen hatched a brood of baby chickens. One afternoon when the little chickens were scattered all over the yard, I suddenly saw the shadow of a hawk overhead. Then I noticed something very unique that taught me a lesson I will never forget. That mother hen did not run to those little chicks and jump on top of them to try to cover them with her wings. No!

Instead she squatted down, spread out her wings and began to cluck. And those little chickens, from every direction, came running *to her* to get under those outstretched wings. Then she pulled her wings down tight, tucking every little chick safely under her. To get to those babies, the hawk would have to have gone through the mother.

When I think of those baby chicks running to their mother, I realize that it is under His wings that we *may* seek refuge— but we have to run to Him. He does not run here and there, trying to cover us. He said, "I have made protection available. You run to Me!" And when we do run to Him in faith, the enemy *will have to go through God to get to us!*

Chapter 5

His faithfulness is a shield and bulwark.
—Psalm 91:4b

It is *God's* faithfulness to His promises that is our shield. It is not just *our* faithfulness! And God is going to be faithful to the promises that He has made.

When the enemy comes to whisper fearful thoughts in your mind, you can ward off his attack by saying, "My faith is strong because I know that *My God* is faithful, and it is *His* faithfulness that is my shield!"

I have this awesome mental picture

of a huge shield out in front of me – completely hiding me from the enemy—and the shield is God Himself. His faithfulness to His promises guarantees us that His shield will remain forever steadfast and available, but whether or not we stay behind the protection of that shield is our choice.

This scripture also tells us that God's faithfulness is our *bulwark*. According to *Nelson's Bible Dictionary*, "a bulwark is a tower built along a city wall from which defenders shoot arrows and hurl large stones at the enemy." Think about that!

God's faithfulness to the promises that He has made is not only a shield, but it is also a *tower* nestled into the hedge of protection that we have around us. From that tower, God is faithful to point out the enemy so he can't slip up on our blind side. Then we are able to use our spiritual weapons to hurl ammunition (God's Word) to stop the schemes of the enemy.

Chapter 6

You will not be afraid of <u>the terror by night..!</u>   —Psalm 91: 5a

Verses five and six cover **every evil known to man**. They are divided into four categories. We will look at those categories one at a time.

The   first   category—**terror   by night**— includes all the evils that come through man: kidnapping, robbery, rape, murder, terrorism, wars…! It is the dread— or horror—or alarm— that comes from what man can do to you. God says, "You will not be afraid of any of those things… because they will not approach you."

Do you realize how many times Jesus told us not to be afraid? Why do you think He continually reminds us not to be afraid? Because it is through faith in His Word that we are protected—and since fear is the opposite of faith, the Lord knows that fear will keep us from operating in the faith that is necessary to receive. No wonder God does not want us to be afraid of the *terror by night.*

So, how do we keep from being afraid? Very simply! Fear comes when we think we are responsible for bringing about this protection ourselves. Too often, we think—"Oh, if I can just believe hard enough, maybe I'll be protected!" That's wrong thinking! **The protection is already there.** It has already been provided, whether we receive it or not. Faith is just the choice to *receive* what Jesus has *already* done.

The answer is in the *Blood of Jesus.* Old Testament believers didn't have as good a covenant as we have on this side of the cross. Yet even under the Old Covenant, Exodus 12: 23 tells us that when Israel put blood on the door facings, the destroyer could not come in. The animal blood they used back then serves as a *type and shadow,* or a picture, of the Blood of Jesus which ratifies our *better* protection—or our *better* Covenant.

When we confess out loud, "I am covered and protected by the Blood of Jesus"—and believe it, the devil literally cannot come in! Remember that verse two tells us, "I will *say* ... the Lord is my Refuge and my Fortress." It is *heart and mouth*— believing with our heart and confessing with our mouth.

Our physical weapons are operated with our hand, but we operate spiritual weapons with our mouth. The Blood is applied by *saying it*—in faith.

Never before in our history has there been so much talk of *terrorism* and *germ warfare,* but to the surprise of so many people—God is not shocked or caught off guard by these things. Do we think *chemical warfare* is bigger than God? Long before man ever discovered biological weapons, God had made provision for the protection of His people—if they would believe His Word.

> And these signs will accompany
> those who have believed...if they
> drink any deadly poison, it will
> not hurt them... —Mark 16:17-18

According to the *Strong's Concordance,* the word *drink* in this scripture comes from the Greek word *to imbibe* which means "to drink, to absorb, to inhale or to take into the mind." No evil has been conceived by man, against which God has not provided a promise of protection for any of His children who will choose to believe it and act on it.

What about the *terror* that has come on mankind regarding our polluted water supplies, foods contaminated by pesticides...? I do not believe that the Word of God is advocating our not using wisdom, but all the precautions in the world cannot protect us from every harmful thing that could be in our food and water. Therefore, God's instruction to bless our food and water before eating is not just some ritual to make us look more spiritual. Rather, it is another provision for our safety, playing an important role in God's protective plan.

> But the Spirit explicitly says that in later times... men will advocate abstaining from foods, which God has created to be gratefully shared in *by those who believe and know the truth.* For everything created by God is good, and nothing is to be rejected, if it is received with gratitude; for it is sanctified by means of the Word of God and prayer.
> —I Timothy 4: 1-5:

> But you shall serve the Lord your God, and He will bless your bread and your water; and He will remove sickness from your midst.
> —Exodus 23: 25

How good our God is! He knew what we had need of — and made provision for it—before we ever asked! For the one *who believes and knows the truth,* blessing the food and gratefully acknowledging the Father's generous provision literally brings about a sanctification or a cleansing of our food and water.

If we find ourselves being afraid of the *terror by night*, that is our barometer to let us know that we are not dwelling and abiding up close to the Lord in the shelter of the Most High and believing His promises. Fear comes in when we are confessing things other than what God has said. When our eyes are not on God, fear will come. But let that fear be a reminder to repent and get back to the place of *faith in what God has promised.*

We walk by faith, not by sight.
—II Corinthians 5: 7

We have to choose to believe His Word more than we believe what we see— more than we believe the attack. Not that we deny the existence of the attack. The attack may be very real, but God wants our faith in His Word to become more of a reality than what we see in the natural.

For example: Gravity is a fact! No one denies the existence of gravity, but just as the law of aerodynamics can supercede the law of gravity, Satan's attacks can also be superceded by a higher law—the law of faith and obedience to God's Word.

David did not deny the existence of the giant, but he refused to compare the giant to himself. Instead he compared the giant to his covenant with God. He knew that Goliath could not succeed in that arena because he was uncircumcised—in other words, he was a man without God's Covenant.

Chapter 7

You will not be afraid of ... the <u>arrow</u> that flies by day.   —Psalm 91: 5b

The second category of evil is the **arrow that flies by day.** An arrow is something that pierces or wounds spiritually, physically, mentally or emotionally.

Arrows are deliberately sent by the enemy and meticulously aimed at the spot that will cause the most damage. They are not shot off at random. They are targeted toward the area in which we have not yet had our mind renewed by the Word of God.

The target could be an area where we

are still losing our temper – or the area where we are still easily offended – or perhaps it is an area where we are still in rebellion or fear!

God tells us in Hebrews 12: 2 that He is the *"author & finisher of our faith."* So if we will trust and rely on God, He will develop our faith and set us free from the sins that so easily bind us. When arrows are sent to wound us spiritually, financially, physically or emotionally, God wants us to ask and believe that He *will pick us up out of harm's way* and deliver us from calamity.

Long before my husband and I had gone full time in the ministry, we owned and operated a soft drink bottling plant that his dad had started the year before Jack was born. Several years before we sold the business, one of the other bottling plants in our area changed management, and the new manager told us that he was going to *spare no expense* in putting us out of business.

He had told the truth! We could never have anticipated how much money he was going to spend trying to fulfill his promise. He literally went all over town placing free vending machines wherever our vendors were located, and storeowners were continually calling us to come and pick up our equipment. Financially, there was no way to compete, especially when he also started product price cutting and flooding the market with advertising.

The outlook in the natural was pretty dismal, but we had something that he didn't have. We had a *covenant* with God, telling us not to be afraid of the *arrows that fly by day*.

And God is faithful. Those arrows— or circumstances—that had looked impossible for us to overcome, finally passed, and our business was left standing long after the competition was gone. The competitor had obviously expected our business to fold quickly under the intense financial pressure, but when we were able to survive longer than he had anticipated, it was *he* who went under financially.

Chapter 8

You will not be afraid of the pestilence that stalks in darkness.   —Psalm 91: 6a

Fear gripped my heart and beads of perspiration popped out on my forehead as I feverishly ran my fingers over what felt like a lump in my body. How I dreaded that monthly self-examination that the doctor had suggested. My fingertips were as cold as ice from the panic that I had worked up just thinking about what I might find, and the turn that my life would take from there.

On that particular day it turned out to be a false alarm, but the dread of what I might find in the coming months was always there. If you also fight fears of fatal diseases then this is the scripture for you to take hold of.

The third category of evil that God names is **pestilence**. This is the only evil He names twice! And since God doesn't waste words, He must have a specific reason why this promise is repeated.

Have you noticed that when a person says something more than once, it is usually because he wants to emphasize that point? God knew the pestilence and the fear that would be running rampant in these end days. The world is teeming with fatal epidemics that are hitting people by the thousands, so He got our attention by repeating this promise.

It's as though God were saying, "I said it in verse three, *but did you really hear Me?* Just to be sure, I am saying it again in verse six—**you do not have to be afraid of the deadly pestilence!**" This is so contrary to the world that we have to renew our thinking before we comprehend the fact that we do not have to be afraid of the sicknesses and diseases that are epidemic in the world today.

When I first started studying this psalm, I remember thinking, "I don't know whether I have the faith to believe these promises!" It stretched my faith until I thought it would snap like a rubber band that was being pulled too tightly.

But God reminded me that faith is not a feeling. Faith is simply *choosing* to believe what He says in His Word. The more I chose to believe God's Word, the more I had a *knowing* that I could trust and rely on it completely.

Heaven and earth will pass away, but
My Words will not pass away.
—Mark 13: 31

Our inheritance is not limited to what is handed down to us genetically from our ancestors. Our inheritance can be what Jesus provided for us if we believe the Word and put it to work in our lives.

> Christ redeemed us from the curse of
> the law having become a curse for us...
> —Galatians 3:13

The pestilence mentioned here in Psalm 91 is spelled out in detail in Deuteronomy 28, and this scripture in Galatians tells us that we are *redeemed* from every curse (pestilence) if we will just believe and appropriate the promise.

In Bible days when they mentioned pestilence, they were thinking of diseases like leprosy. Today we have diseases like AIDS, cancer, heart disease... but no matter what pestilence we might be facing, His promise is still true. Praise God for His precious promises!

Chapter 9

You will not be afraid of the <u>destruction</u> that lays waste at noon.   —Psalm 91: 6B

This fourth category of evil is **destruction**. Destruction takes in the evils over which mankind has no control—those things that the world ignorantly calls *acts of God*: tornadoes, floods, fire, car wrecks… God very plainly tells us that we are not to fear destruction. These natural disasters are not coming from God.

In Mark 4: 39, Jesus rebuked the storm and it became perfectly calm, demonstrating that God is not the author of such things—otherwise, Jesus would never have contradicted His Father by rebuking something sent by Him.

DID YOU KNOW THAT EVERY EXTREME EVIL KNOWN TO MAN WILL FALL INTO ONE OF THESE FOUR CATEGORIES: TERROR BY NIGHT, ARROWS, PESTILENCE, OR DESTRUCTION? AND THE AMAZING THING IS THAT GOD HAS OFFERED US DELIVERANCE FROM THEM ALL!

Without Psalm 91 we might feel rather presumptuous if, on our own, we prayed *asking* God to protect us from all the things covered in these four categories. In fact, we probably would not have the nerve to ask for all of that, but God is so good. **He offered this protection to us before we even had a chance to ask!** It was God's plan to provide protection for His children even before the foundation of the world.

He said, "You will not be afraid of *terror, arrows, pestilence or destruction* because I have said in My Word that *it will not approach you,* if you are obedient to verses one and two to dwell in My shelter and abide in My shadow." And, of course, we cannot dwell and abide in Him apart from Jesus. But praise God! Because of the shed Blood of the cross, it is now possible.

We can receive anything that God has already provided. The secret is knowing that *everything for which God has made provision* is clearly spelled out and defined in the Word of God. **If you can find where God has offered it—you can have it!** It is never God holding it back. His provision is already there—waiting to be received.

Faith is not a tool to manipulate God into giving you something *you* want. Faith is simply the means by which we accept what God has already made available.

Our goal needs to be the *renewal* of our minds to such an extent that we have more faith in God's Word than in what we see. God does not make promises that are out of our reach.

When the Lord first began showing me these promises, and my mind was struggling with doubt, He took me to a portion of His Word that helped to set me free.

> What then? If some did not believe, their unbelief will not nullify the faithfulness of God, will it? May it never be! Rather, let God be found true, though every man be found a liar, as it is written: that thou mightiest prevail when thou art judged. —Romans 3: 3-4

God is telling us that even though there may be some who don't believe, their unbelief will never nullify His promises to the ones who do believe. A very important part of that verse in Romans 3 is the reminder, in a quote from the Old Testament, that what we as individuals choose to believe and confess will determine our own individual judgment.

Chapter 10

A thousand may fall at your side and ten thousand at your right hand; but it shall not approach you.   —Psalm 91: 7

What an awesome statement! God wants us to know that even though there will be *a thousand falling by our side and ten thousand at our right hand*, it does not negate the promise that destruction will not approach the one who chooses to believe and trust His Word. The *Amplified Bible* says, "…it shall not approach you **for any purpose**". He means exactly what He says.

But it is no accident that this little statement is tucked right here in the middle of the psalm. Have you noticed how easy it is to become fearful when disaster starts striking all around you? We begin to feel like Peter must have felt as he walked on the water to Jesus. When he suddenly started seeing all the turbulence of the storm going on around him, it is easy to see how he started sinking with the waves.

God knew there would be times when we would hear so many negative reports and see so many needs around us that we'd feel overwhelmed. That's why He warned us ahead of time that thousands would be falling all around us. He didn't want us to be caught off guard.

But at that point, we have a choice. The ball is in our court! We can choose to run to His shelter in faith, and it will not approach us—or we can go the way of the world.

What tremendous insight after our minds have been renewed by the Word of God to realize, contrary to the world's thinking, that we do not have to be among the ten thousand who fall at our right hand.

Too many people see Psalm 91 as a beautiful promise that they file right along side all of their other good quality reading material—and it makes them feel comforted every time they read it. But I don't want anyone to read this book and fail to see the *superior significance* to these promises in this psalm.

Psalm 91 is the *preventive* measure that God has given to His children against every evil known to mankind. No other promise in the Bible offers this total protection for living in this world. It is the *health formula* to ward off every evil before it has time to strike. This is not just a *cure*—it is a *total prevention*!

Jesus says in Matthew 5: 18, *"not the smallest letter or stroke of His Word will pass away until it is all accomplished."* Thank God that even though we may have read over these promises for years and failed to appropriate their worth, the truth never passed away or lost its power.

Late one night, soon after building our new home in the country, we were faced with a severe weather alert. The local radio station was warning that a tornado had been sited just south of the Country Club—the exact location of our property. We could see several of the React Club vehicles parked on the road below our hill as the members watched the funnel cloud that seemed to be headed straight for our house.

I had never seen such a strange, eerie color in the night sky or experienced such a deafening silence in the atmosphere. You could literally feel the hair on your body standing on end. Some of our son's friends were visiting and to their surprise, Jack quickly ordered our family to get outside with our Bibles and start circling the house—reading Psalm 91 and taking authority over the storm.

The eerie silence suddenly turned into a roar, with torrents of rain coming down in what seemed like buckets rather than drops. Finally, Jack got a peace that the danger had passed, even though nothing by sight had changed.

However, we walked back into the house just in time to hear the on-location radio announcer exclaim with so much excitement that he was almost shouting, *"This is nothing short of a miracle—the funnel cloud south of the Country Club has suddenly lifted back in the sky and vanished before our very eyes."*

You should have seen those kids jumping and hollering and slapping one another on the back. For many of them, it was their first time to see the supernatural at work.

Their surprise, however, was no greater than that of the professor the next day when he asked the students what they were doing during the storm. Several said that they were in the bathtub under a mattress—some were in closets—one was in a storm cellar!

When he finally got around to our daughter, Angelia, you can imagine the astonishment when she said, "With the tornado headed our direction, my family was circling the house, quoting from Psalm

91—— *"We will not be afraid of the destruction that lays waste! Because of the Blood of Jesus, it will not approach us."*

You will only look on with your
eyes, and see the recompense of
the wicked. —Psalm 91: 8

Faith in God and in His Son Jesus Christ and His Word is counted in God's eyes as righteousness. But when we are in unbelief—to a degree, we are placing ourselves in the category of the *wicked*. Sometimes, even as a Christian, I have been an *unbelieving* believer when it comes to receiving *all* of God's Word.

Many people think of the Gospel as an insurance policy, securing just their eternity. They are depriving themselves of so much. Perhaps we all need to ask ourselves the question, "What kind of coverage do I have—fire or life?" God's Word is more than just an escape from hell. It is a handbook for living a victorious life in this world.

For you have made the Lord, my
refuge, even the Most High,

your dwelling place.
　　　　　　　　—Psalm 91: 9

Verse nine just emphasizes again *our part* of the covenant. It is as though God were saying, "Remember now, this *Psalm 91 walk of faith* does not come automatically. Making the Lord your refuge and your place of safety and continually dwelling in His Presence by making Him your total Source is what makes it possible."

Chapter 11

No evil will befall you, nor will any
plague or calamity come near your dwelling.
—Psalm 91: 10

After God repeats our part of the
condition in verse nine, He then re-
emphasizes the promise in verse 10: "No
evil (none of the four categories of evil)
will befall you, nor will it come near your
dwelling place (your household)."

God has just added a new dimension
to the promise. The opportunity to exercise
faith, not only for yourself but also for the
protection of your entire household, is now
being given to you.

If these promises were only available to us as individuals, it would not be all that comforting. God has created us with an instinct to want to be protected, but He has also placed within us an innate need to protect those who belong to us. That is why He is assuring us here that these promises are for you *and your household*.

It appears that the Old Testament leaders had a better understanding of this concept than we who are under the New Covenant. That is why Joshua chose for himself *and for his household*.

> If it is disagreeable in your sight to serve the Lord, then choose for yourselves today whom you will serve; but as for me *and my house*, we will serve the Lord.
> —Joshua 24: 15

As Joshua made the decision that his household would serve God with him, he was at the same time influencing their destiny and declaring their protection. In much the same way, Rahab bargained with the Israeli spies for her whole family.

You will not be afraid of evil tidings
because your heart is steadfast—
trusting in His Word. —Psalm 112:7

When our hearts are truly steadfast in
Him and when we are trusting in His faithfulness to fulfill His promises, we'll not be
constantly afraid that something bad is going to happen to one of our family members. Negative expectations will begin to
pass away and we will start expecting
good reports.

Several years ago as I was cooking
breakfast, Jack walked into the kitchen with
one of the glands under his chin so swollen
that it looked as though he had attempted to
swallow a large soft ball that had lodged on
one side of his throat. I rushed him to this
close physician friend of ours and I thought
I could tell by the expression on the doctor's face that he was concerned. But when
the first words out of his mouth were, "I am
going to call in another doctor to have a
look at you," all doubt was removed and I
then knew he was concerned that there was
something seriously wrong.

Typically, the enemy tried to unload a whole carload of fear thoughts and fear pictures in my mind before they had even gotten out of the room, but when God's Word has been stored in the heart it has a way of surfacing just when it's needed. This scripture in Psalm 91: 10: "No evil will befall you, nor will any plague or calamity come **near your dwelling**" was more than just a *comforting* thought. It brought *life* and *hope* to the situation.

I sat there in the waiting room thanking God for this promise and rejoicing over the outcome long before the doctor ever poked his smiling face around the corner to tell me that everything was fine. It turned out to be just a sore throat that had settled in the gland on one side of Jack's throat. Even the swelling had gone down by the next morning.

I thank God for this added dimension of being able to apply *His Covenant Umbrella of Protection* for our entire household. What a joy to know that your family is safe.

Chapter 12

For He will give His angels charge concerning you, to guard you in all your ways.
They will bear you up in their hands, lest you
strike your foot against a stone.—Psalm 91: 11-12

Here in verses 11-12 God makes another unique promise concerning an additional dimension of our protection. This is
one of the most precious promises of God,
and He put it right here in Psalm 91. Most
Christians read past this promise with very
little, if any, thought about the magnitude
of what is being said. Only after we get to
heaven will we realize all the things from
which we were spared because of the inter-
vention of God's angels in our behalf.

I am sure you have read stories about missionaries whose lives were spared because would-be murderers saw large body guards protecting them—when, in fact, there was no one there in the natural. And we can all recall close calls where we escaped a tragedy, and there was no explanation in the natural. Not only is it possible *"to entertain angels without knowing it"* like it says in Hebrews 13:2, but sadly, I believe most Christians have a tendency to disregard the ministry of angels altogether.

A friend of ours, who was working in the mines in Clovis, New Mexico, had the job of setting off explosives. One particular day he was ready to push the switch when someone tapped him on the shoulder. To his surprise no one was any where around. Deciding that it must have been his imagination, he started once again to push the switch, when he felt another tap on his shoulder. Again, no one was there, so he decided to move all the ignition equipment several hundred feet back up the tunnel. When he finally set off the explosion, the whole top of the tunnel caved in exactly where he had been standing. Coincidence?

You could never make our friend believe that.

This verse 11 says, "For He will give His angels *charge* concerning you!" What does that mean? Well, think with me for a moment! Have you ever *taken charge* of a situation? When you take charge of something, you put yourself in a place of leadership, and you begin telling everyone what to do and how to do it.

If angels are taking charge of the things that concern us, that means that God has given the angels, *not the circumstances*, the authority to act on our behalf. That same truth is repeated in Hebrews.

> Are they (angels) not all ministering spirits, sent out to render service for the sake of those who will inherit salvation?
> —Hebrews 1: 14

When we look to God as the Source of our protection and provision, the angels are constantly *rendering us aid* and *taking charge* of our affairs.

Verse 11 also says "angels will *guard* you in all your ways." Have you ever seen a soldier stand guard over someone to protect them? That soldier stands at attention: alert, watchful and ready to protect at the first sign of attack. How much more will God's angels stand *guard* over God's children, alert and ready to protect them at all times? Do we believe that? Have we ever even thought about it? Faith is what releases this promise to work in our behalf.

Angelic protection is just another one of the *unique* ways in which God has provided for the protection of His children.

Chapter 13

You will tread upon the lion and cobra, the young lion and the serpent (dragon in the KJV) you will trample down.   —Psalm 91: 13

Here in verse 13 God transitions to another topic. He takes us from the subject of our being protected *by Him*, and He begins putting emphasis on *the authority* in His Name that has been given to us as believers.

Make a note of the corresponding New Testament scripture that deals with the authority that has been given to us:

Behold, I (Jesus) have given you authority to tread upon serpents

and scorpions, and over all the
power of the enemy, and nothing
shall injure you. —Luke 10:19

We, as Christians, have been given
authority over the enemy — *he does not
have authority over us!* We need to take
the time to allow that fact to soak in! However, our authority over the enemy is not
automatic.

My husband says that too many
Christians *take authority* when they should
be *praying*, and they *pray* when they
should be *taking authority!* For the most
part Jesus prayed at night and took authority all day. When we encounter the enemy,
that is not the time to start praying. We
need to be already prayed up. When we encounter the enemy, we need to be speaking
forth the authority that we have in the
Name of Jesus.

If a gunman suddenly faced you,
would you be confident enough in your authority that you could boldly declare, "I am
in Covenant with the Living God, and I
have a Blood Covering that protects me

from anything that you might attempt to do. So in the *Name of Jesus*, I command you to put down that gun!"

If we do not have that kind of courage, then we need to meditate on the authority scriptures until we become confident in who we are *in Christ*. At new birth we immediately have enough power placed at our disposal to tread upon the enemy without being harmed. But most Christians either don't know it or they fail to use it. How often do we believe the Word enough to act on it?

What does the Word mean when it says, "We *will tread on the lion, the young lion, the cobra, and the dragon?"* This is just a metaphorical look at things that are potentially harmful in our daily lives. These terms are just a figurative way of describing the different types of problems that come against us. So what do these terms mean to us today? Let's break them down.

First of all, there are **"lion problems"** — those problems that are bold, loud and forthright — problems that come out in the open and hit us face on. At one time or another, we have all had something come against us that was blatant and overt. It might have been a car wreck, or a boss who chewed us out royally in front of our fellow employees. Or it might have been an unexpected bill at the end of the month that caused a chain reaction of checks bouncing. Those are *lion* problems—obvious problems that often seem insurmountable and yet God says that we will tread on them—they will not tread on us.

The **"young lions"** can grow into full-grown problems if we don't handle them. These young lion problems come against us to harass and destroy gradually—like little foxes!

Catch the foxes for us, the little foxes that are ruining the vineyards, while our vineyards are in blossom.
—Song of Solomon 2: 15

Next God names **"cobra** problems." These are the problems that seem to sneak up on us like a *snake in the grass* when we are going through our day, minding our own business. They are what we might call an *undercover* attack that brings sudden death—like a deceptive scheme that keeps us blinded until it devours us.

The previous figurative examples we might have guessed, but what are the *dragon* problems? I looked that Hebrew word up in the *Strong's Concordance* and it listed "sea monster." First of all,—there is no such thing as a dragon or a sea monster. Dragons are a figment of one's imagination. Have you ever experienced fears that were a figment of your imagination? Sure you have! We all have!

Dragon problems represent our unfounded fears—phantom fears or mirage fears. That sounds harmless enough, but are you aware that they can be as deadly as the real fears—if we believe them?

Some people's *dragon* fears are as real to them as another person's *lion* problems. That is why it is important to define your fears. So many people spend all of their lives running from something that is not even chasing them.

But the *Good News* is—God says that we will tread on *all* of the powers of the enemy — no matter whether they are loud and bold, sneaky and deceptive or just imaginary fears. God has given us authority over all of them!

No longer are we to put up with the paralyzing fears that at one time gripped our hearts and left us powerless at the sight of the evil that was striking all around us. God has given us His *Power of Attorney* and these problems now have to submit to the authority that has been given to us in His Name.

Chapter 14

Because he has loved Me, therefore
I will...   —Psalm 91: 14a

In verses 14-16 the psalm moves
from talking in third person about God's
promises, to God speaking to us personally
and declaring promises in first person. It is
the Voice of God speaking prophetically to
each one of us. In these three verses He
gives seven promises. (Seven is the Hebrew
number for completion.) Take special note
of the fact that **these seven promises are
reserved for those who love Him**.

First of all, we need to ask ourselves, "Do I really love Him?" This is

much like Jesus when He asked Peter, *"Peter, do you love Me?"* (John 21: 15) Can you imagine how Peter must have felt when Jesus questioned him three times, "Peter, do you love Me?" Even so, we need to question ourselves because these promises are made only to those who have genuinely set their love on Him.

And remember that the Lord said in John 14:15, *"If you love Me, you will obey Me!"* Our obedience is an extremely good *telltale* sign that shows us that we really love Him. Do you love Him**? If you do, these promises are for you!**

Chapter 15

Because he has loved Me, therefore <u>I will deliver him</u>... Psalm 91: 14a

A promise of deliverance is the first of the seven promises made to the one who loves God. Make it personal! For instance, I quote it like this: "Because I love You, Lord, I thank You that You have promised to deliver me." Then we need to ask ourselves, *"From what is He going to deliver me?"*

God will deliver us from *all* of the following:

- The lion problems

* The young lion problems
* The cobra problems
* The dragon problems
* The terror by night (evils that
    come through man)
* The arrows that fly by day —
    (wounds)
* The pestilence—(plagues,
    fatal epidemics)
* The destruction—(evils over
    which man has no control)

In other words, God wants to deliver us from every evil known to mankind. What a promise. I thank God that He is the God of deliverance!

Nothing is impossible with God!
—Luke 1: 37

Chapter 16

Because he has loved Me...<u>I will set him securely on high,</u> because he has known My Name.   —Psalm 91: 14B

To be set securely on high is the second *promise* to those who love the Lord and know Him by Name. "It is My Name," God says, "that has been on his lips when he faces troubles, and he has run to Me. He has called out to Me in faith; therefore, I will set him on high."

> ...which He brought about in Christ, when He raised Him from the dead, and seated Him at His right hand in the heavenly places, far above all rule and authority

and power and dominion and every name that is named, not only in this age, but also in the one to come...and raised us up with Him, and seated us with Him in the heavenly places, in Christ Jesus.
—**Ephesians 1: 20-21; 2:6**

In verse 14 the word *known* from the Old Testament, according to *Strong's Exhaustive Concordance,* means *"to have knowledge of"* or *"to be acquainted with."* Most people under the Old Testament only had knowledge *about* God—they just had an *acquaintance* with Him. However, Hebrews 8: 11, quoting from the Prophet Jeremiah who was speaking of the New Covenant that was to come, uses a different word *know* to describe our knowledge of God today.

The New Testament Greek word *know* according to the *Strong's Exhaustive Concordance* means *"to stare at, to discern clearly, to experience and to gaze at something remarkable with wide open eyes."* When God refers to our *knowing* Him today, He is referring to something much more personal than they experienced in the

Old Testament. This promise of being seated securely on high is for the one who *experiences God intimately.*

What does verse 14 mean when it says that we have known *His Name*? Interestingly, under the Old Covenant when God wanted to reveal something more about Himself or when He wanted to reveal another portion of His Promise, He would introduce Himself by another one of His Covenant Names.

For example, in Genesis 22:14, when God introduced Himself to Abraham as the *Provider,* He did so by revealing His covenant name *Jehovah-jireh* which means, "I am the Lord who provides." Progressively through the Old Covenant, God introduced Himself by new names, each one revealing a new segment of His Character and of His precious promises.

Read this verse in first person. "Lord, You have promised that You will set me securely on high because I have known Your Name on a first hand basis. I have experienced Your Covenant Promises brought forth in your different Covenant Names."

Jehovah-Jireh:
The Lord our Provider

Jehovah-Rapha:
The Lord our Healer

Jehovah-Shalom:
The Lord our Peace

Jehovah-Tsidkaynoo:
The Lord our Righteousness

Jehovah-Raah:
The Lord our Shepherd

Jehovah Shammah:
The Lord Ever Present

Jehovah-Nissi:
The Lord our Banner

This is by no means a complete list, but just an example of how God has always revealed Himself, His Character, and His Promises *through His Name*. God says that the promises are ours — because we *know His Name*.

> There is no other name under heaven that has been given among men, by which we must be saved (healed, delivered, protected, sustained)–Acts 4: 12

Chapter 17

He will call on Me, and <u>I will answer</u>
<u>him</u>...   —Psalm 91: 15 a

God makes a third promise here in
verse 15 that He will *answer* those who
truly love Him and call on His Name. Are
we aware of what a wonderful promise God
is making to us here when He says that He
will answer those who call in His Name (in
His will)?

> And this is the confidence which we
> have before Him, that, if we ask any
> thing according to His will, He hears
> us. And if we know that He hears us
> in whatever we ask, we know that we
> have the requests which we have ask
> ed from Him.   —I John 5: 14–15

Nothing gives me more comfort than to realize that every time I pray in line with God's Word, He hears me. And if He hears me, I know I have the request for which I asked. This one promise keeps me continually searching His Word in order to understand His will and His promises so that I can know how to pray more effectively.

Don't give in –even for a moment — to the doubts and fears that will come to your mind at times. If we continue to stand fast in faith, He will remain faithful to what He has promised.

> Let us hold fast the confession of hope without wavering, for He who promised is faithful!
> —Hebrews 10:23

The enemy may try to cause sudden surprises to catch us unaware and knock us down. But God is faithful, and His Word is true—no matter what the circumstances look like at times.

Recently my husband decided to change insurance companies to get a lower premium and that, of course, was going to require a physical examination for both of us. The young nurse came to our house early one morning and began taking blood work, electrocardiograms (EKGs), blood pressure checks.... the whole nine yards!

Weeks went by after that with no word from the company, in spite of the numerous phone calls that we made trying to get the results. They kept assuring us that it just took time to get all of the papers in order, so we finally decided to wait patiently for the test results.

Several months later when checking our mail, my husband and I discovered a packet marked "Notice: policy enclosed". It was our insurance. Happy to finally have that out of the way, I opened the envelope to file the policy, but to my surprise a check fell out of the envelope returning half of our premium.

The letter read, "We are sorry to inform you that we cannot insure your wife as she did not pass the health exam. If you would like further details, please fill out the enclosed form." For just a moment I think my heart skipped a beat. The devil was screaming in my ear, "Facts are facts! You have something wrong with you that is serious enough to be refused insurance coverage, and you don't even know what it is."

For the next few minutes, panic tried to overtake me. Every fearful thought imaginable was flooding my mind. Was there something in the blood work? Maybe something was found in the EKG! Half a dozen possibilities flooded my mind.

It was then that I had to be honest with myself. I realized that for weeks I had been pushing back and ignoring a subtle anxiety that had kept the door open to an uneasiness in my emotions. Fear can be such a subtle enemy.

It was at this point that I had a mother-daughter talk with Angelia. But it was *she* who was giving *me* advice—instead of the other way around. A little tender loving care and sympathy would have been welcome, but instead, my daughter gave me what I needed to hear, rather than what I wanted to hear. Her words rang loud and clear — "when you are walking with God and trusting in His Word, then to entertain reasoning and fear is sin — so stop it. Don't go there!"

Her message was short and to the point, but it accomplished what I needed. It put me back on track. Even though a person may have a revelation of a Truth of God, there are times when circumstances seem so overwhelming that they temporarily distract us and overshadow the Truth. Thank God for someone who loves us enough to call us back to the reality of God's Word!

A quality decision *not to go there in my mind*— by refusing to even consider some of the negative possibilities concerning my health — finally put those fears to flight. Whenever a negative thought tried to come, I simply said, "A thousand may fall at my side and ten thousand at my right hand, but God's Word says that it will not approach me for any purpose—so I refuse to go there in my thinking!"

My peace had returned long before the medical report finally came in showing an irregularity in my EKG. I was so thankful that I had already made my decision not to allow my mind to go into reasoning. Otherwise, it would have been a big temptation to give in again at the sound of that report. But every time a negative thought came, I would quote Psalm 91, using the words *heart problems* for *pestilence*.

Finally another EKG was scheduled with a heart specialist, and this time the report showed that it was something so minor that it required neither medication nor even a follow-up visit. As I sat there that afternoon praising God for the second EKG report, I couldn't help but shudder to think what I might have opened myself up to without the promise of Psalm 91 and without the determination to refuse to entertain fearful thoughts.

What we allow our mind to dwell on is *our* choice. Therefore, if we desire to operate in this protection covenant, taking authority over negative thoughts and emotions is imperative. It is amazing how the simple phrase, *"I am just not going there,"* will dispel those fears immediately.

Chapter 18

...I will be with him in trouble; <u>I will res-</u>
<u>cue him</u>...   —Psalm 91: 15

The fourth Promise *to rescue from trouble* those who love the Lord is found in the middle of verse 15.

It reminds me of a story that I read about a U.S. Senator during the pre-Civil War days that was said to be a true story. The Senator had taken his son to the slave market, and the boy noticed a black mother crying and praying as they were preparing to sell her daughter on the slave block. As he walked closer, he overheard the mother crying out, "Oh, God, If I could help You as easily as You could help me, I'd do it for You, Lord." The young man was so touched by the prayer that he went over and bought the girl off the slave block and gave her back to her mother.

God answers our prayers and rescues us in so many different ways. I am so thankful that He is creative and not limited by our seemingly impossible situations. But we have to ask in faith and not confine Him to our limited resources. God says, "If you love Me (if you are faithfully obedient to Me), I will be with you when you find yourself in trouble, and I will rescue you." But we have to trust Him to do it *His* way.

> When you pass through the waters,
> I will be with you; and through the
> rivers, they will not overflow you.
> When you walk through the fire,
> you will not be scorched, nor will
> the flame burn you.   —Isaiah 43:2

Agnes Sanford told a true story about a friend of hers. The friend had a son in the war zone in World War II, and she wrote out Psalm 91 and sent it to him. She explained that Psalm 91 would be his protection. The son took it to his commanding officer who assigned his whole outfit to read the entire psalm out loud together every morning. She said that when the war was over—this was the only outfit in the war zone that reportedly had not one casualty.

Our son, Bill, who is pictured on the front cover with his wife, Sloan, and their two children, Cullen and Meritt, saw the *rescuing* power of God when he found himself in serious *trouble* after attempting to swim across a lake—that was much wider than he calculated. With no strength left in his body and having already gone under twice, Bill experienced all the sensations of a drowning person. But miraculously, God not only provided a woman on the opposite, previously deserted bank, but also enabled her to throw a life ring (that just *happened* to be nearby) over 30 yards, landing within inches of his almost lifeless body.

Some people might call happenings like these a coincidence, but the negative situations that we encounter can become *God-incidences* when we trust His Word.

Chapter 19

...I will <u>honor</u> him.   —Psalm 91: 15

The fifth Promise to *honor* those who love God is in the last part of verse 15.

All of us like to be honored. I can remember the teacher calling my name when I was in grade school and complimenting a paper I had turned in. That thrilled me. I was honored.

Several years ago our daughter, Angelia, and her husband, Dr. David Schum, attended a political rally in our city that was given for George W. Bush when he was campaigning for Texas Governor. She had shared a quick anecdote with him at the beginning of the meeting when they first met. After he had spoken and was leaving with some of his colleagues, everyone was shocked when he left his group and darted back to our daughter to say, "Remember the promise I made —no tears for you in November." It honored her that he not only remembered her, but also recalled their conversation.

Each year we honor the man who is chosen *outstanding man of the year* in our city. Civic organizations give plaques every year to honor men and women who have made exceptional contributions. It's an honor, and it feels good to have someone we consider important pay special attention to us. It is a thrill to be honored by man, but how much more of a tribute and a thrill when we are honored by God. Fulfilling our part of the Covenant enables God to honor us.

Have you ever thought about what it means to be honored by the God of the Universe? He honors us by calling us His sons and daughters. He honors us by answering when we take His Word seriously and call out to Him in faith. He honors us by recognizing us individually and by preparing a place for us to be with Him eternally. *Giving us honor* is one of the seven unique promises made in Psalm 91.

Chapter 20

<u>With a long life I will satisfy him.</u>
—Psalm 91: 16a

The sixth promise *to satisfy* those who love Him with a long life is found in verse 16.

God does not just say that He will prolong our lives and give us a lot of birthdays. No! He says that He will *satisfy* us with a long life. There are people who would testify that just having a great many birthdays is not necessarily a blessing. But God says that He will give us many birthdays, and as those birthdays roll around we will experience satisfaction.

It has been said that there is a *God shaped vacuum* on the inside of each one of us. Man has tried to fill that vacuum with many different things, but nothing will satisfy that emptiness until it is filled with Jesus. That is the true satisfaction to which God refers in His Promise.

God is making the offer. If we will come to Him, let Him fill that empty place on the inside and allow Him to fulfill the call on our lives—then He will give us a long life and satisfy us as we live it out. Only the dissatisfied person can really appreciate what it means to find satisfaction.

Chapter 21

...and let him <u>behold My Salvation</u>.
—Psalm 91: 16 b

To allow those who love Him to *behold His salvation* is the seventh promise found in the last part of verse 16. *Behold* simply means *to take hold of.* God wants us to take hold of His salvation.

Many people are surprised when they look up the word *"salvation"* in a Bible concordance and find that it has a much deeper meaning than just *a ticket to heaven.* We often miss the richness of this promise.

According to *Strong's Exhaustive Concordance,* the word *salvation* includes health, healing, deliverance, protection and provision. What more could we ask? God promises that He will allow us to *take hold of* His Health, His Healing, His Deliverance, His Protection and His Provision!

Summary

Nothing in this world can be relied upon as confidently as God's promises when we believe them and refuse to waver—when we decide to make His Word *our final authority* for every area of life.

I believe that Psalm 91 is a covenant (a contract) that God has made available to His children—especially in these difficult days. But there are some who sincerely ask, "How do you know that you can take a *song* from the Psalms and base your life on it?" Jesus answered that question. The value of the Psalms was emphasized when He cited them as a source of Truth that must be fulfilled.

> Now He said to them, "These are My words which I spoke to you while I was still with you, that all things which are written about Me in the law of Moses and the Proph ets *AND THE PSALMS* must be fulfilled." —Luke 24: 44

When Jesus specifically equated the Psalms to the law of Moses and the Prophets, we see that it is historically relevant, prophetically sound and totally applicable.

At a time when there are so many uncertainties facing us, it is more than comforting to know that God not only knows ahead of time what we will be facing, but He also made absolute provision for us.

It seems only a dream now to think back on the time when my mind was reeling in fears and uncertainties. Little did I know when I asked God that pertinent question –"Is there any way for a Christian to escape all the evils that are coming on this world?"—that He was going to give me a dream that would not only change my life, but also change the lives of hundreds of others who would hear and believe.

Someone once said, "It is interesting that the world must have gotten its distress 911 number from God's answer to our distress call —Psalm "91-1".

Our minds cannot even begin to comprehend God's goodness. **TRULY, WHAT A MIGHTLY GOD WE SERVE.**

What must I do to be Saved?

The promises from God in this book are for God's children who love Him. If you have never given your life to Jesus and accepted Him as your Lord and Savior, there is no better time than right now.

> There is none righteous, not even one.
> —Romans 3: 10

> ...for all have sinned and fallen short of the glory of God.   —Romans 3: 23

God loves you and gave His life that you might live eternally with Him.

> But God demonstrates His own love toward us, in that while we were yet sinners, Christ died for us.
> —Romans 5: 8

> For God so loved the world (you), that He gave His only begotten Son, that whoever believes in Him should not perish but have eternal life.   —John 3: 16

There is nothing we can do to earn our

salvation or to make ourselves good enough to go to heaven. It is a free gift!

> For the wages of sin is death, but
> the *free* gift of God is eternal life
> in Christ Jesus.   —Romans 6: 23

There is also no other avenue through which we can reach heaven, other than Jesus Christ—God's Son.

> And there is salvation in no one else;
> for there is no other name under hea
> ven that has been given among men,
> by which we must be saved.–Acts 4:12

> Jesus said to him, "I am the way, and
> the Truth, and the Life; no one comes
> to the Father, but through Me."
>   —John 14: 6

You must believe that Jesus is the Son of God, that He died on the cross for your sins, and that He rose again on the third day.

> ...who (Jesus) was declared with
> power to be the Son of God by
> the resurrection from the dead…
>   —Romans 1: 4

You may be thinking, "How do I accept

Jesus and become His child?" God in His Love has made it so easy.

> If you confess with your mouth the Lord Jesus and believe in your heart that God raised Him from the dead, you shall be saved. —Romans 10: 9

> But as many as received Him, to them He gave the right to become children of God, even to those who believe in His Name. —John 1: 12

It is as simple as praying this prayer—if you sincerely mean it in your heart:

Dear God:
I confess that I am a sinner. I deserve to go to hell. But I believe that Jesus died for me, that He shed His Blood to pay for my sins and that You raised Him from the dead so that I can be Your child and live with You eternally in heaven. I am asking Jesus to come into my heart and save me this very moment.
I thank You dear Lord for loving me and saving me.
In Jesus Name,
Amen

**Testimony by Jennifer McCullough
25 year old Howard Payne University graduate
currently serving as a Preteen Minister
in Dallas, Texas,
while working on her Masters in Education
at Southwestern Baptist Theological Seminary**

Before leaving for East Africa in 1999, I was being discipled by Angelia Schum, my college Bible study teacher. It was a crash course in *Everything you need to know before entering "the Bush!"* I ran into her friend Donna Crow one night at church. She said, "You do know about Psalm 91, don't you?" When I said, "No!"—she said, "Angie must not love you very much if she hasn't told you about Psalm 91!"

I began intently studying the chapter and memorized it before I left. I had no idea the power this passage has until January 15th, 2000. I lived in a village in the bush with the Ankole tribe (cattle herders), working with orphans with AIDS and teaching at the village school. I often found myself praying Psalm 91 while walking the circumference of the village. I had gone to the city the day before on the milk truck. That night I was lying in my hut and heard gunshots. I ran to a fellow missionary's hut and sat in a small room praying Psalm 91 over and over. The husband was out investigating, so it was just a 24 year old mother, her 2 year old child and me.

In the meantime, a group of rebels were raiding my village. Men were shot, a pregnant woman was beaten, villagers were robbed and cattle were stolen. The villagers were laid out in a line on their stomachs with guns and machetes pointed to their heads, while they were being threatened not to say a word. The raid was well planned as they had been watching the village for days from the bushes.

Here is the miracle! Village people know that white missionaries have more in their huts than Ugandans make in a lifetime. Yet the rebels never came to our hut—in spite of the fact that everyone else's hut was raided. After the fact, the rebels admitted to the police that they had followed the milk truck through the bush the night before the raid. I had been on that truck sitting next to the driver who was carrying two million shillings—the villagers' monthly income from the milk sales. They did not attack the truck in route because we had returned before dark that night. This was the first time we had ever returned before dark in the six months I had been riding it.

The day after the attack, it was very intense. I walked through the village praying for villagers who had been robbed and beaten. They had looks of pure terror on their faces, knowing that the rebels were still hiding in the bush nearby. While talking to the villagers, no one could believe that I was not attacked. My interpreter, Segambe, said, "It was as if your hut was not even there."

God is faithful! He has a perfect plan for your life!

God is all knowing! He will give you weapons to fight the battles you face.

God did not give Psalm 91 only to missionaries in the African bush. He gave it to everyone so that we can daily claim His promises to us as Christians. I find the words of Psalm 91 in my daily prayers: "...He will cover you with His feathers, and under His wings you may find refuge. His faithfulness will be your shield and rampart..."

Don't miss the chance to see the power of God's promises in your life. Claim them, memorize them, pray them, and live them. He is faithful!

Julie's Miracle as told by her father
Dr. James Crow—dentist in Brownwood, Texas

Julie's ordeal began in May, 1983, while attending a friend's birthday party in the country. Julie had ridden horses with her grandfather for almost nine of her ten year life, so when they asked who wanted to ride she jumped at the chance. But a ten year old riding bare back on a grown horse has very little to hold onto—so when the horse began to run she slipped under its belly. And between the rocks and the hooves she received a very serious head injury.

When we arrived at the hospital a physician friend tried to be a buffer for us before we saw our daughter. He warned us that she was in very serious condition and that the hospital was already making arrangements to have her transported to the nearest large city for treatment. Even with his attempt to prepare us, we were still not anywhere close to being prepared for what we saw. The right side of her head was swollen literally the size of a volleyball, both eyes were swollen shut and her hair and face were drenched in blood. There was no way we could have recognized her.

I need, at this point, to interject some crucial information. Through the teachings of Kenneth Copeland of Copeland Ministries in Ft Worth, I had started doing a great deal of study on healing and faith. Jesus and I had spent a lot of time alone together during which time I had received the baptism of the Holy Spirit and the Lord had become very personal to me. Our church was strong on believing that Jesus had made healing available to us if we only believed.

I can truly say that from the instant I first saw her condition, I called on Jesus and totally expected that His healing power and His promises in Psalm 91 would bring her through. I'm glad I didn't have to analyze the situation, but we all knew it was so bad that we had to have a miracle. Before the ambulance reached the hospital, a growing network of believers were interceding for Julie and for us.

In addition to the driver, there were two paramedics in the back of the ambulance with Julie and one in the front between the driver and me. I prayed all the way—just in a whisper—almost oblivious to the others in the cab. I remember thanking Jesus for her healing and telling satan that he couldn't have Julie—that she was a child of God and had been dedicated to the Lord from birth. For the entire eighty-five miles, I never stopped claiming her healing. I didn't yell! I didn't cry! I knew Jesus could hear me, and I knew satan could hear me.

Somewhere just short of the city, the paramedics slid open the panel between the back and the cab area and said something to the driver. We had been going fairly fast all the way, but at this point the driver put on his siren and sped the rest of the way to the hospital.

I found out later that the paramedics had informed the driver that Julie had lost all vital signs and could not be revived. I'm not sure how long she had no vital signs, but it was more than minutes. I learned that life came back into her body about the time we came to the edge of town.

While all this was happening, my brother-in-law who was an elder in our church was about forty-five minutes behind us in his car. On the way he felt that God told him that Julie had died, and God asked him if he would be willing to lay across her body like the prophet Elisha had done with the little boy in II Kings 4: 34 to bring him back to life. Realizing this meant he would most likely have to push his way past the doctors and nurses and look very foolish, he said that he wrestled with himself for several minutes before knowing without a doubt that he was willing to do it. The moment the commitment was made, he felt God told him Julie would be all right.

We later backtracked to the place where he was en route during this confrontation with God. According to our calculations—the ambulance would have been coming into the city limits just about the time God told him that Julie would be all right. That was when her vital signs had returned.

My wife and sister got there while Julie was having a CAT scan, so I was the only one who had been able to attempt to communicate with her. Even though I got no response from her, I told her I loved her and that she would be OK.

After the doctor got the results of the CAT scan, he gave us no hope whatsoever. Someone had asked him if there would be brain damage, and he replied, "Parents always want to ask about brain damage. Your concern needs to be whether or not she will live through the night, but if she does live—yes, there will be extensive brain damage."

He was not arrogant and neither was I. But I denied each negative statement from anyone who was not standing in faith with us. The doctor was obviously perturbed with us, but I'm sure he just thought we were in denial. He just didn't realize where our denial was coming from.

To the doctor's total surprise, Julie did live through the night. We kept healing scriptures on her pillow at all times and held her and spoke love to her continuously. My wife had the astronomical job of cleaning the dried blood from her hair and untangling it— speaking healing and quoting Psalm 91 over her the whole time.

We were informed we were in for a long stay, but my frustration was that she wasn't climbing out of the bed the next day—ready to go home. God must have given me a *gift of faith* because I was ready for a Lazarus healing. Miraculously, we began to notice that nearly every timetable we were given was accomplished seven times faster. At first we thought it was a neat coincidence, until it continued way beyond any possibility of happenchance.

During the hospital stay of only nine days, we saw our miracle unveil. The physical damage continued to heal at the supernatural rate. Swelling went down, color returned to normal, mental behavior went from the bizarre back to normal— every day was a miracle. There were other patients in the hospital with head injuries, seemingly not nearly as serious as Julie's, who had been there six months and more—and many of them were just learning how to walk and talk again.

During the next few days after the accident, we saw Julie protected by Jesus while He was accomplishing her healing. It was as if her body were left on the hospital bed to go through the healing while Julie herself—her soul maybe, for sure her spirit—seemed to retreat inside to be cuddled by Jesus until the healing process was complete. For the first several days, we could not recognize anything about her that reminded us of our Julie. Then a little at a time we saw her return until she was totally back to normal. We could almost see the healing taking place before our very eyes. The nurses were amazed. They all called her their "miracle girl".

Even our hardcore neurosurgeon—without giving credit to God—said that her recovery couldn't be explained. He saw us praying and standing and believing day after day, and because of the results before his very eyes, he could not very easily have gone home and called us a bunch of kooks.

On the night of the accident we had been told that in addition to the brain damage, there would be considerable loss of hearing since the mastoid bone had been part of the skull fracture. They were also quite sure that the optic nerve had been damaged—which we were told would cause either total, or at least partial, loss of eye sight.

When Julie was dismissed only nine days after entering the hospital, the only outward sign of the accident was some blood shot still in her right eye. But she went home with no brain damage and no loss of eye sight (20-20 vision). On the day of her release, however, the attending physician—even after watching her miraculous recovery—still insisted, "There will be a hearing loss," and he instructed us to take her to the audiologist in July. We did that, only to be told that she had perfect hearing.

We thank Jesus for what He did on the cross for each and every one of us and for the wonderful promises that He has made to us in Psalm 91.

Audra Chasteen, a member of the Living Word Church in Brownwood, Texas, gave in her own words this testimony—following a spectacular demonstration in the life of her son, Skylar, of God's faithfulness to fulfill His promises in Psalm 91.

About 7:30 in the evening on July 28, 2001, three of my sisters and I, along with our children, were visiting my parents. Skylar, my four year old, was riding bicycles with the older boys out in the pasture about a half mile from the house. I had just turned to warn my older son not to ride down the hill because of the steep incline, when I realized that Skylar had already started down. The next thing I knew the bicycle was out of control and he had gone over the side of a cliff. I was the first one to reach him, and he wasn't

moving and he wasn't crying. He was tangled in the wheel of the bicycle, lying on his stomach with his chin past his shoulder, resting on his shoulder blade. It was a terrifying sight to see Skylar's head twisted backwards. His left arm was back behind him with his wrist above his right shoulder. His eyes were half open, but in a fixed position down and to the corner. He was blue and he was not breathing.

When I saw Skylar in that distorted position and not breathing, I didn't have to be told that it was bad. I just started screaming. In spite of the obvious head and neck injury, I turned his head forward so that he could breathe. But when he still didn't start breathing—I turned his whole body straight, hoping that would help. When that didn't work, I became hysterical. My three sisters and I are nurses, one RN and three LVNs, but we couldn't seem to pull ourselves together to know what to do medically. It was as though none of us had one brain cell functioning. My sister Donna just picked him up and stood there holding him.

When my oldest sister, Cynthia, finally got to the scene of the accident, the first thing she did was to lay her hand over on Skylar's head and start rebuking the enemy. She kept saying, "I rebuke you, satan, in the Name of Jesus—you get your hands off Skylar—you cannot have him!" Then she started pleading the Blood of Jesus and quoting Psalm 91 over him. Hearing God's Word coming out of Cynthia's mouth pulled me back to my senses. I sent one of my sisters for her car, and we headed for the nearest hospital—which was about seventeen miles away. Another sister was calling 911, but it would have been at least an hour before they could have even found us.

On the way to the hospital we did some rescue breaths on Skylar, and he would breathe for a few minutes and then stop. I tried to hold his head and neck straight, but the whole time his eyes were still fixed. Cynthia and I continued to speak Psalm 91 over Skylar and to command his body to line up with God's Word—but nothing was coming out as eloquently as I wanted. All that I could say was, "Bones, be like you're supposed to be—Body, be like you're supposed to be—in Jesus' Name."

I remember thinking—"God, how can you ask us to praise You in *every* situation—how can I praise you when my child is in danger?" And I felt like the Lord impressed me, "Just do it—you don't have to know why—just do it!" I was able to give God one sentence—"Lord, I give you the Glory and the Honor and the Praise." (I wasn't giving God the praise from thinking that He sent this situation—I was giving God the praise because of *who He is* and because His Word said to praise Him in the midst of all things.) The whole way we prayed in the Spirit and kept quoting Psalm 91 over him.

When we got to the hospital in Comanche,

Texas, they immediately put a neck brace on him, but he still wasn't responding. By then he had started breathing on his own, but his eyes were still fixed. Then he started throwing up—another sign of a bad head injury.

As soon as they had Skylar in X-ray, I called one of our pastors to get some of the intercessors praying. I knew we needed help. As much as we had been taught, I was still unprepared when the tragedy actually happened. As he prayed, peace came over me and I suddenly knew that everything was going to be OK.

The X-rays showed an obvious break in the C-1 vertebra (the first vertebra under the head) and Skylar still wasn't responding. The physicians put him, with the X-rays, on an air-flight to Cook's Children's Hospital in Fort Worth, Texas.

Since I was still in my scrubs from working all day, they didn't realize at Cook's Hospital that I was the mother, so they had me helping to draw the blood on Skylar. I was listening as the trauma nurse reported to the doctor when he came in –"he has a C-1 fracture, his eyes are deviated and down to the left, he stopped breathing, etc." The doctor was shocked when he discovered I was the mother. I could never have been that peaceful if it had not been for the prayers.

The only thing that seemed to calm Skylar while we were waiting was to put my hand on his forehead and pray Psalm 91 over him. Even though Skylar was not awake through all of this, once when I paused in my praying Skylar said, "Amen!" From the moment that he responded from an unconscious state—giving his agreement to that prayer—I knew he would be fine, in spite of the seriousness of his condition. Finally they wheeled him in for more X-rays and for a CT scan to see if there was any bleeding in the brain cavity .

When the doctor finally came in he had a very strange look on his face, and all he could say was, "He's going to be all right!" Then after his consultation with the Radiologist, they came in saying, **"We don't know how to explain this but we can find no head trauma (brain swelling or bleeding) and we cannot find a C-1 fracture."** They had the Comanche hospital X-rays with the obvious break, but their X-rays showed no sign of a break.

There are no words to describe the joy and the gratitude and the excitement that we felt at that moment. All the nurses were pouring in to tell us how *lucky* we were and all I could say was, "Luck had nothing to do with this. This was God!" I was not about to let satan have one ounce of glory. I knew that it was a miracle and that it was God who had healed him, however, he still wasn't responding very well so they put us in the pediatric ward of the ICU to monitor him. The next morning the nurse came in and scratched him on the head, assuming she would get the same response (nothing) that she had gotten the day before. But this time when she scratched him and called out his name he said, "What?" Everyone, including the nurse, jumped – and then rejoiced!

From that point on he was able to wake up and respond. The doctor was just amazed. He said, "I don't know what to tell you. There was definitely a break on that other X-ray, but he is obviously OK now. I don't know how to explain it." He didn't have to explain it. I knew what had happened. God is so good!

Skylar has always been very close to my mother, and I found out something very interesting after we got home. Two weeks prior to the accident, Sklar had been telling her that it was time for him to go be with Jesus. And mother would say, "No, Skylar, why would you say that? It's not time for you to go be with Jesus." But he would emphatically say, "Yes, it is! I've got to go" And she would argue with him, but she said she didn't think too much about it since he's only four years old. But after the accident my mother knew that there was warfare going on, and it was God's promise in Psalm 91 that finally won the battle.

Since the day we walked out of the hospital, Skylar has been a perfectly normal, healthy little boy. He has had no problems and no side effects from the accident. He is truly a miracle!

Psalm 91 Testimony from Nazi Prison Camp

Many people came to know and trust the Lord during World War II. One was an Englishman who was held in a German prison camp for a long period of time. One day he read Psalm 91.

"Father in heaven," he prayed, "I see all these men dying around me, one after the other. Will I also have to die here? I am still young and I very much want to work in Your kingdom here on earth."

He received this answer: "Rely on what you have just read and go home!"

Trusting in the Lord, he got up and walked into the corridor toward the gate. A guard called out, "Prisoner, where are you going?"

"I am under the protection of the Most High," he replied. The guard came to attention and let him pass, for Adolf Hitler was known as "the Most High."

He came to the gate, where a group of guards stood. They commanded him to stop and asked where he was going.

"I am under the protection of the Most High." All the guards stood at attention as he walked out the gate.

The English officer made his way through the German countryside and eventually reached England, where he told how he had made his escape.

He was the *only one* to come out of that prison alive.

Testimony taken from Corrie ten Boom's book: *Clippings from My Notebook*

My Personal Psalm 91 Covenant Prayer